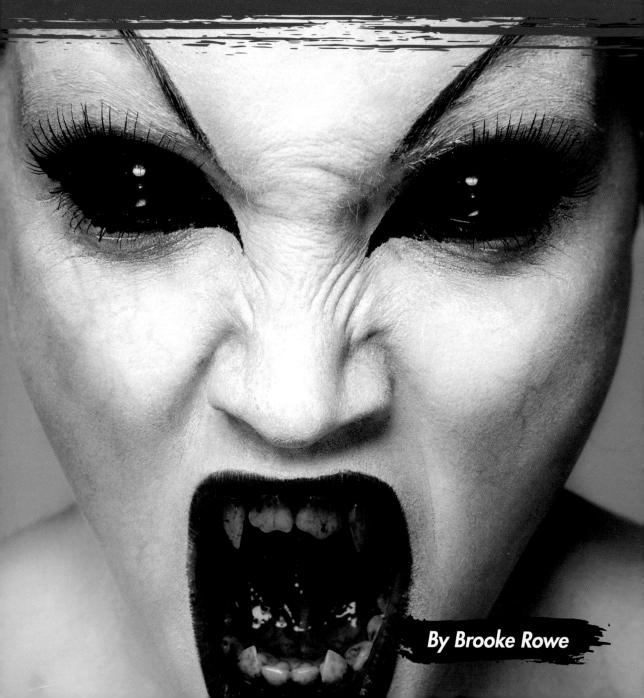

WHAT MONSTER ARE YOU MOST LIKE?

By Brooke Rowe

Published in the United States of America by Cherry Lake Publishing
Ann Arbor, Michigan
www.cherrylakepublishing.com

Reading Adviser: Marla Conn, ReadAbility, Inc.
Book Designer: Melinda Millward

45th Parallel Press is an imprint of Cherry Lake Publishing.

CIP data has been filed and is available at catalog.loc.gov.

Printed in the United States of America
Corporate Graphics

Table of Contents

Introduction

Hey! Welcome to the Best Quiz Ever series. This is a book. Duh. But it's also a pretty awesome quiz. Don't worry. It's not about math. Or history. Or anything you might get graded on. Snooze.

This is a quiz all about YOU.

To take the Best Quiz Ever:

Answer honestly!
Keep track of your answers. But don't write in the book!
(Hint: Make a copy of this handy chart.)
Don't see the answer you want? Pick the closest one.
Take it alone. Take it with friends!
Have fun! Obviously.

Question 1 _____   Question 7 _____

Question 2 _____   Question 8 _____

Question 3 _____   Question 9 _____

Question 4 _____   Question 10 _____

Question 5 _____   Question 11 _____

Question 6 _____   Question 12 _____

To get a copy of this activity, visit
www.cherrylakepublishing.com/activities.

Your friends say you:

A. Have a really nice smile

B. Are always loyal

C. Should get more sleep

D. Never look good in photographs

Did you know?
In 2015, a man was arrested for pretending to be a dentist. He pulled five teeth from someone for no reason.

Which foreign country would you like to visit?

A. Romania

B. France

C. Cuba

D. England

Did you know?

Romanian gymnast Nadia Comaneci got the first perfect score in gymnastics in the 1976 Olympics. She was 14 years old.

Who's the coolest actor?

A. Robert Pattinson

B. Tyler Posey

C. Nicholas Hoult

D. I don't do movies

Did you know?

Nicholas Hoult dated Jennifer Lawrence. She played Katniss in The Hunger Games.

Which of these things is the most annoying?

A. Garlic

B. Silver jewelry

C. People with too much energy

D. Crossing large rivers and lakes

Did you know?
Garlic is poisonous to cats and dogs.

Which kind of music is weird but kind of awesome?

A. Classical

B. 1980s pop

C. Folk music

D. Opera

Did you know?
Josh Groban sings "popera," which
is a mix of pop and opera.

What's one of your bad habits?

A. Staying up too late

B. Having messy hair

C. Overeating

D. Sneaking up on people

Did you know?
Randy Gardner holds the record for
the longest time without sleep—
11 days and 24 minutes!

Which of these seems the least scary to you?

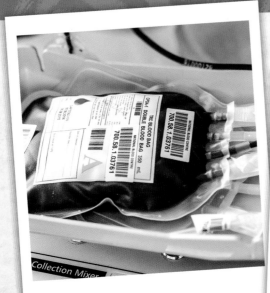

A. Blood

B. The woods at night. Alone.

C. Zombie **apocalypse**

D. Being invisible

Did you know?
O-positive is the most common blood type in the United States.

The best birthday celebration would be:

A. An all-night party

B. Camping with friends

C. A giant food fest

D. Laser tag

Did you know?

Americans eat 100 acres (40.5 hectares) of pizza a day. That's about 350 slices per second!

You're waiting in the park for a friend. You:

A. Need sunglasses. And a hat.

B. Chase squirrels

C. Zone out

D. Hide. And wait to scare him.

Did you know?
Your eyeballs can get sunburned just like your skin.

Which of these would be the most awesome pet?

A. Bat

B. Coyote

C. Ant farm

D. White tiger

Did you know?
Because of their **genes**, many white tigers are cross-eyed.

Where would be the greatest place to live?

A. A castle in the mountains

B. A cabin in the woods

C. A tropical island

D. An empty mansion

Did you know?
The Venetian Las Vegas has 7,117 hotel rooms, more than any other hotel.

Which TV show is your favorite?

A. Vampire Diaries

B. Dog Whisperer

C. *Monster High*

D. *Scooby-Doo*

Did you know?

Scooby-Doo first aired in 1969. That was
the same year as the moon landing!

Solutions

You're done! Now you tally your score. Add up your As, Bs, Cs, and Ds. What letter do you have the most of? BTW, if you have a tie, you're a little bit of both.

As: Vampire

I vant to suck your blood! You love to stay up late. And sleep in. Mornings are a total bummer. When you do roll out of bed, you usually put on black. From head to toe. Some call you a loner. Some of your best friends are animals. Bats. Wolves. The smell of garlic makes you barf. But a nice, rare steak makes you drool. Are you sure you aren't a vampire?

Bs: Werewolf

Ah-ooooooooo! You're actually a werewolf! You love running around outside. Especially if your other options are school or chores. Camping. Hiking. Chasing rabbits. You just like fresh air. You have a close group of friends. Your teachers call your group "the wolf pack." And you always look out for your pack. Night is your favorite time. But be careful under a full moon!

Cs: Zombie

Must . . . eat . . . brains . . . You're a zombie. You tend to zone out at the worst moments. Like when homework is being assigned. And you're usually pretty sleepy. Unless there's food around! You and your best friends can gulp down entire pizzas. And sometimes brains. American zombie stories say you're from the Caribbean. So book your next vacation at the beach. And try not to bite anyone!

Ds: Ghost

Boo! You're a ghost! Are you sure you're even here right now? You have a **rebellious** streak. You usually do whatever you want. And what you want depends on the day of the week! Sometimes you play nasty tricks. Sometimes you help your friends out. Your friends say you move as quietly as a cat. Just don't try to walk through walls. You'll get hurt!

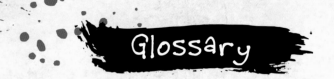
Glossary

apocalypse (uh-POK-uh-lips) a great disaster

Cuba (KYOO-buh) an island country in the West Indies

garlic (GAHR-lik) a plant that has a strong smell and is used in cooking

genes (JEENS) parts of cells that control the appearance of a living thing

opera (AH-pur-uh) a story set to music

rebellious (rih-BEL-yuhs) tending to fight against the people in charge of something

Romania (roh-MAY-nee-uh) a country in southeastern Europe on the Black Sea

Index